Good Science—*That's Easy to Teach*

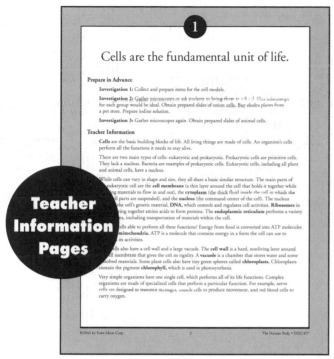

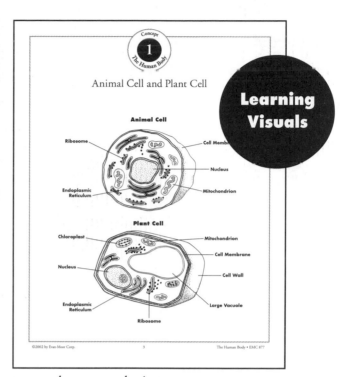

Teacher Information Pages

Learning Visuals

- the concept to be studied
- items to obtain or prepare in advance
- background information

- reproduce or make into transparency

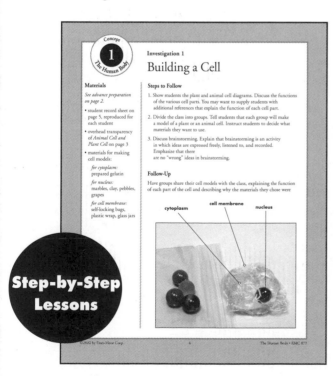

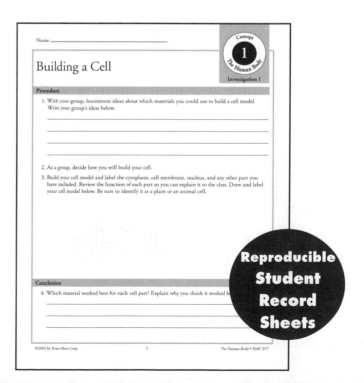

Step-by-Step Lessons

Reproducible Student Record Sheets

Cells are the fundamental unit of life.

Prepare in Advance

Investigation 1: Collect and prepare items for the cell models.

Investigation 2: Gather microscopes or ask students to bring them to school. One microscope for each group would be ideal. Obtain prepared slides of onion cells. Buy elodea plants from a pet store. Prepare iodine solution.

Investigation 3: Gather microscopes again. Obtain prepared slides of animal cells.

Teacher Information

Cells are the basic building blocks of life. All living things are made of cells. An organism's cells perform all the functions it needs to stay alive.

There are two main types of cells: eukaryotic and prokaryotic. Prokaryotic cells are primitive cells. They lack a nucleus. Bacteria are examples of prokaryotic cells. Eukaryotic cells, including all plant and animal cells, have a nucleus.

While cells can vary in shape and size, they all share a basic similar structure. The main parts of the eukaryotic cell are the **cell membrane** (a thin layer around the cell that holds it together while allowing materials to flow in and out), the **cytoplasm** (the thick fluid inside the cell in which the other cell parts are suspended), and the **nucleus** (the command center of the cell). The nucleus contains the cell's genetic material, **DNA,** which controls and regulates cell activities. **Ribosomes** in the cell string together amino acids to form proteins. The **endoplasmic reticulum** performs a variety of functions, including transportation of materials within the cell.

How are cells able to perform all these functions? Energy from food is converted into ATP molecules in a cell's **mitochondria.** ATP is a molecule that contains energy in a form the cell can use to power all its activities.

Plant cells also have a cell wall and a large vacuole. The **cell wall** is a hard, nonliving layer around the cell membrane that gives the cell its rigidity. A **vacuole** is a chamber that stores water and some dissolved materials. Some plant cells also have tiny green spheres called **chloroplasts.** Chloroplasts contain the pigment **chlorophyll,** which is used in photosynthesis.

Very simple organisms have one single cell, which performs all of its life functions. Complex organisms are made of specialized cells that perform a particular function. For example, nerve cells are designed to transmit messages, muscle cells to produce movement, and red blood cells to carry oxygen.

Animal Cell and Plant Cell

Animal Cell

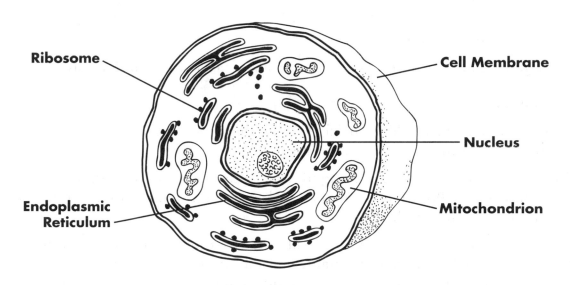

Ribosome

Cell Membrane

Nucleus

Endoplasmic Reticulum

Mitochondrion

Plant Cell

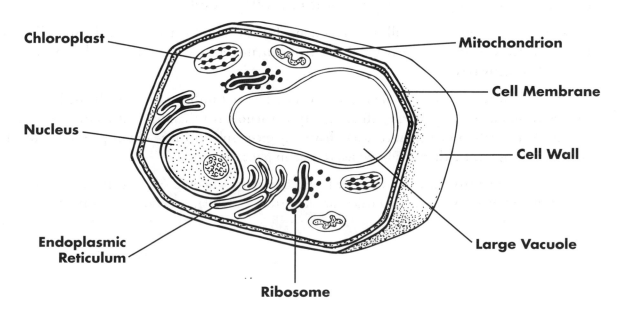

Chloroplast

Mitochondrion

Cell Membrane

Nucleus

Cell Wall

Endoplasmic Reticulum

Large Vacuole

Ribosome

Investigation 1

Building a Cell

Materials

See advance preparation on page 2.

• student record sheet on page 5, reproduced for each student

• overhead transparency of *Animal Cell and Plant Cell* on page 3

• materials for making cell models:

  for cytoplasm: prepared gelatin

  for nucleus: marbles, clay, pebbles, grapes

  for cell membrane: self-locking bags, plastic wrap, glass jars

Steps to Follow

1. Show students the plant and animal cell diagrams. Discuss the functions of the various cell parts. You may want to supply students with additional references that explain the function of each cell part.

2. Divide the class into groups. Tell students that each group will make a model of a plant or an animal cell. Instruct students to decide what materials they want to use.

3. Discuss brainstorming. Explain that brainstorming is an activity in which ideas are expressed freely, listened to, and recorded. Emphasize that there are no "wrong" ideas in brainstorming.

Follow-Up

Have groups share their cell models with the class, explaining the function of each part of the cell and describing why the materials they chose were appropriate.

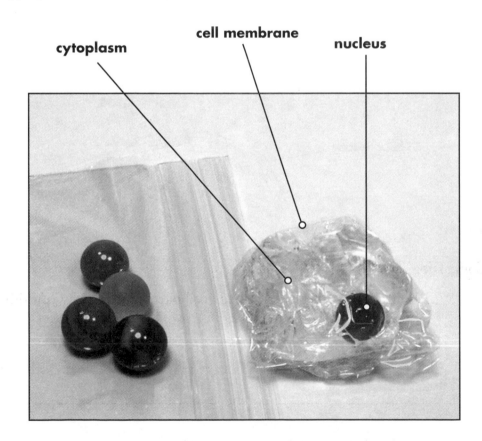

cytoplasm   **cell membrane**   **nucleus**

Building a Cell

Procedure

1. With your group, brainstorm ideas about which materials you could use to build a cell model. Write your group's ideas below.

   _____

   _____

   _____

   _____

2. As a group, decide how you will build your cell.

3. Build your cell model and label the cytoplasm, cell membrane, nucleus, and any other part you have included. Review the function of each part so you can explain it to the class. Draw and label your cell model below. Be sure to identify it as a plant or an animal cell.

Conclusion

4. Which material worked best for each cell part? Explain why you think it worked best.

   _____

   _____

   _____

Investigation 2

Looking at Plant Cells

Materials

See advance preparation on page 2.

- student record sheet on page 7, reproduced for each student
- overhead transparency of *Animal Cell and Plant Cell* on page 3
- microscope for each group
- slides
- cover slips
- iodine solution or other stain
- pieces of onion bulb
- elodea plants
- tweezers
- toothpicks
- water
- newspaper

Steps to Follow

1. Prepare an iodine solution by mixing one part iodine to four parts water. You may also use methylene blue, eosin, or food coloring. Have students cover their work tables with newspaper.

2. Explain to students that all living things are composed of cells. Tell them that today they will be looking at plant cells under the microscope. Show them the plant cell transparency. Explain that all (eukaryotic) cells have cytoplasm, a nucleus, and a cell membrane, while plant cells also have a hard, nonliving layer around the membrane called a cell wall. Tell students that green plants also contain chloroplasts, green structures that contain a substance (chlorophyll) plants use to make their own food from water, carbon dioxide, and sunlight.

3. Arrange the class into groups of three or four with a microscope and materials for each group.

4. Instruct students to use the tweezers to peel a small, very thin piece of onion from just below the skin of the bulb and place it on the slide. Explain that stains emphasize the different parts of the cell so they can be seen more easily. Have students use a toothpick to add a bit of stain to the onion piece. Finally, have them gently place a cover slip on top.

5. Tell students to place the slide on the microscope stage and adjust the focus until they can see the onion cells. Have students draw what they see on their record sheets.

6. Instruct students to prepare another slide with a piece of elodea leaf on it. After observing it under the microscope, students should record their observations.

7. Have students describe how both types of cells looked under the microscope.

Follow-Up

Students should notice that the elodea cells had green chloroplasts while the bulb cells did not. Discuss with students why this might be. (Onion bulb cells are not exposed to light and so do not photosynthesize.)

Looking at Plant Cells

Procedure and Observations

1. Place a thin layer of onion bulb on your slide and stain it.

2. Look through the eyepiece of your microscope and adjust the mirror until your field of vision is very bright. Turn the arm or focus knob so that the microscope stage is at the farthest position from the lower lens. Place the slide on the stage. While looking through the eyepiece, slowly turn the focus knob until you can see the onion cells clearly.

3. Draw what you see in the first circle below. Label the cell wall, nucleus, and other cell parts that you see.

4. Repeat this procedure using a small piece of the elodea leaf. Draw and label what you see in the second circle.

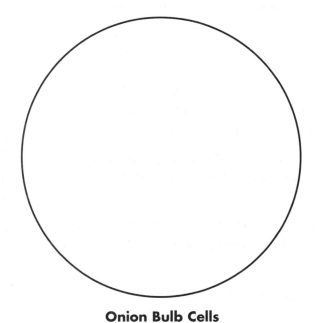

Onion Bulb Cells

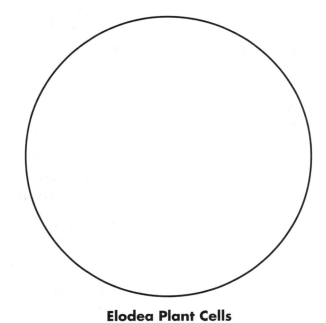

Elodea Plant Cells

Conclusion

5. Do all plant cells look the same? Explain.

_____

_____

_____

Concept **1** The Human Body

Investigation 3

Looking at Animal Cells

Materials

See advance preparation on page 2.

- student record sheet on page 9, reproduced for each student

- overhead transparency of *Animal Cell and Plant Cell* on page 3

- microscope for each group

- prepared slides of animal cells (cheek cells, nerve cells)

Steps to Follow

1. Discuss the difference between plant and animal cells. Talk about the onion and elodea cells and how they looked under the microscope. Tell students that today they will be looking at prepared slides of animal cells.

2. Show students the animal cell transparency. Remind students that all (eukaryotic) cells have cytoplasm, a nucleus, and a cell membrane.

3. Arrange the class into groups of three or four, each with a microscope and materials.

4. Instruct students to place the prepared slide on the microscope stage and adjust the focus until they can see the animal cells. You may need to assist students with the microscopes.

5. Have students draw what they see on their record sheets.

6. Instruct students to look at another prepared slide. After observing it under the microscope, students should record their observations on their record sheets.

7. Ask students to describe what the animal cells looked like under the microscope.

Follow-Up

Have the class make a chart comparing the plant and animal cells they observed. Explain that although these cells look different, they all have some things in common: a nucleus, cytoplasm, and a cell membrane.

If possible, get some live one-celled animals to view under the microscope. Paramecium are probably the best to look at. They are not as slow as amoebas, nor as fast as euglenas. These organisms may be purchased through any biological supply company. Explain that these one-celled animals perform all the functions that our specialized cells do: ingestion of food and oxygen, excretion of waste products, reproduction, etc.

Looking at Animal Cells

Procedure and Observations

1. Look through the eyepiece of your microscope and adjust the mirror until your field of vision is very bright. Turn the arm or focus knob so that the microscope stage is at the farthest position from the lower lens.

2. Choose a prepared slide of an animal cell. Place the slide on the stage. While looking through the eyepiece, slowly turn the focus knob until you can see the specimen clearly.

3. Illustrate what you see in the first circle. Label the cell membrane, nucleus, and other cell parts that you see.

4. Repeat this procedure using a slide of a different type of animal cell. Draw what you see in the second circle.

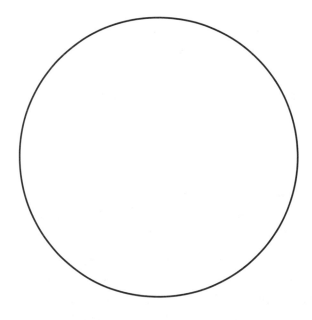
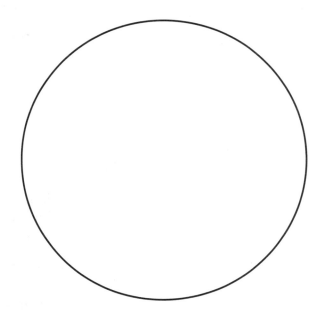

_____   _____

Conclusion

5. Do all animal cells look alike? Explain.

_____

_____

_____

             The Human Body • EMC 877

2

Specialized cells protect the body from harmful substances.

Prepare in Advance

Investigation 1: Purchase a loaf of bread, preferably one without preservatives.

Investigation 2: Purchase enough apples so that each group can have two. Make sure the apples have unbroken skins.

Teacher Information

Most **microorganisms** (microbes) are neither plant nor animal. Instead, they belong to the kingdoms Protista, Monera, and Fungi. They include viruses, amoebas, bacteria, algae, and fungi. Some are harmless and even helpful. But others, called **pathogens,** can cause infectious diseases.

Bacteria cause strep throat, whooping cough, and meningitis. **Viruses** are responsible for polio, influenza, and mumps. **Fungi** cause ringworm and athlete's foot. Infectious diseases are spread through the air or water, or by direct contact from one organism to another.

Fungi include molds, yeasts, and mushrooms. They are not plants, because they can't make their own food. Instead, they get food by living off other organisms. Fungi produce microscopic reproductive cells called **spores** that float around in the air. When the spores land on food, and the conditions are right, they can reproduce, causing the food to spoil.

The body has many defenses against disease. Skin, nose hair, mucus, and body acids work to block infectious materials from entering the body. If these devices fail, the body's immune system makes **antibodies** that kill the invading germs.

Microbes

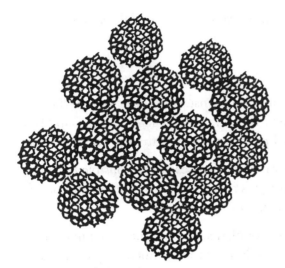

Polio virus

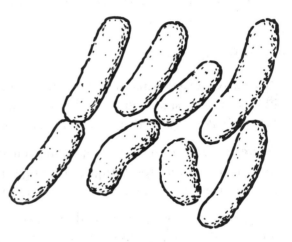

Rod-shaped *Bacilli* bacteria

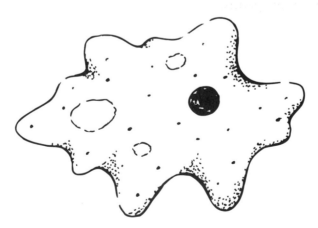

An amoeba is a protist.

Investigation 1

Peeking at Pathogens

Materials

See advance preparation on page 10.

- student record sheet on page 13, reproduced for each student
- slices of bread, preferably without preservatives
- trays to hold materials
- water
- self-locking bags
- labels
- paper towels
- hand lenses

Steps to Follow

1. Place students in groups of four and give each group a tray of materials. Have students contaminate the bread by rubbing it gently on the floor or sink area. Students should then break the bread in half, moisten half, and leave the other half dry.

2. Have students place each piece of bread in a self-locking bag, label the bags "wet" or "dry," and place their bags on the tray. Label the tray with the names of group members.

3. Store all trays in a warm, dark place.

4. Students should observe their bags with a hand lens every three or four days for a two-week period. Have them describe their observations on their record sheets. ***Caution: Under no circumstances should students open the bags. Some students might be allergic to the mold.***

5. Have students continue to illustrate and describe their observations throughout the two-week period. Students might see spots of different colors. Explain that each spot is a colony of mold and that all the organisms in each colony are the same kind of mold.

6. Explain what molds are and how they grow. Point out that in this investigation students examined a mold that grew on bread, but that some kinds of molds can grow on people too! Locker room users are cautioned to keep their feet dry to avoid athlete's foot, a fungal condition that is often a problem in the damp environment of a locker room.

Follow-Up

Do molds grow in all environments? Repeat the experiment, placing the trays in different parts of the room (warm and sunny, dark and cold).

Name _____

Peeking at Pathogens

Procedure and Observations

1. Follow your teacher's instructions for setting up two bags of contaminated bread.

2. Put the labeled bags of contaminated bread in a warm, dark place.

3. Observe both bags with a hand lens every few days for a two-week period. **Do not open the bags.** Record your observations below.

Day	Dry Bread Observations	Wet Bread Observations
1		
3		
6		
9		
11		
14		

Conclusion

4. Did mold grow better on the wet or dry bread? Support your answer with evidence from your experiment.

_____

_____

_____

_____

_____

Investigation 2

Skin Shield

Materials

See advance preparation on page 10.

- student record sheet on page 15, reproduced for each student
- trays to hold materials
- apples
- pins
- labels
- self-locking bags
- large box
- hand lenses

Steps to Follow

1. Remind students that some microorganisms (viruses, amoebas, bacteria, and fungi) can cause infectious diseases.

2. Discuss the body's barriers against disease: the skin, nose hair, and enzymes that prevent infectious materials from entering the body.

3. Tell students that they will do an investigation to determine how the skin prevents pathogens from entering an organism.

4. Place students in groups of four and give each group a materials tray. Students should use the pin to score the surface of one apple and then rub the scored apple on the floor or other dirty surface. They should then put the apple in a self-locking bag and label the bag "broken skin."

5. Tell students **not** to puncture the second apple but to rub it gently (so as not to break the skin) on the floor, and place it in another self-locking bag. This bag should be labeled "unbroken skin."

6. Get a large box. After labeling both bags with a group name or other identifier, have each group put their apples in the box. Place the box in a warm place.

7. After a week, have students observe the apples with a hand lens. **Students should not open the bags.** Have them dispose of the apples in their bags once they have completed their observations.

Follow-Up

Have students repeat the experiment using different fruits and vegetables. In each case, they should prepare a "broken skin" sample and an "unbroken skin" sample. The unbroken skin sample will act as a control in their experiment.

Name _____

Skin Shield

Investigation 2

Procedure

1. Score the skin of the first apple, rub it on an unclean surface, put it in a self-locking bag, and label the bag "broken skin."

2. Rub the second apple gently (so you don't break the skin) on an unclean surface. Put it in a self-locking bag and label the bag "unbroken skin."

3. Place the bags in a warm place.

Observations

4. After a week, observe the apples with a hand lens. **Do not open the bags.** Draw and color what you observe. Describe your observations on the lines.

Broken-skin Apple   **Unbroken-skin Apple**

_____   _____

_____   _____

_____   _____

_____   _____

Conclusion

5. Based on your observations, what can you conclude about skin's role in protecting an organism from disease?

_____

_____

©2002 by Evan-Moor Corp.   15   The Human Body • EMC 877

Food follows a path as it is digested.

Teacher Information

When stretched out end to end, the digestive system of an adult can reach the height of a four-story building. It fits inside the body because it's folded up around itself. The body cannot live without the energy from food, but it cannot use food in its original form. It must first break down the food into a simpler form. Food is broken down mechanically and chemically as it moves through the **digestive system.**

Digestion begins in the mouth. There, the teeth break food into smaller pieces. Saliva contains an enzyme that breaks down starch into sugar. From the mouth, food moves toward the stomach via the **esophagus,** a long tube that connects the mouth and stomach.

Although we speak of food moving "down" to the stomach, it isn't gravity that pushes the food along. Instead, circular muscles in the esophagus contract behind the food mass and lengthwise muscles push the food forward. This process is called **peristalsis.**

In the stomach, gastric juice and other enzymes continue to break down the food.

Food then moves into the small intestine where most digestion takes place. Enzymes produced by the pancreas and liver are secreted into the small intestine where they act to digest the food. The pancreas secretes pancreatic juice, which digests starch, fat, and protein. The liver produces bile, which breaks down fat.

Digested food enters the bloodstream through the walls of the small intestine. Blood carries the digested food to all parts of the body. Undigested food goes to the large intestine, and is eventually carried out of the body through the anus.

The Digestive System

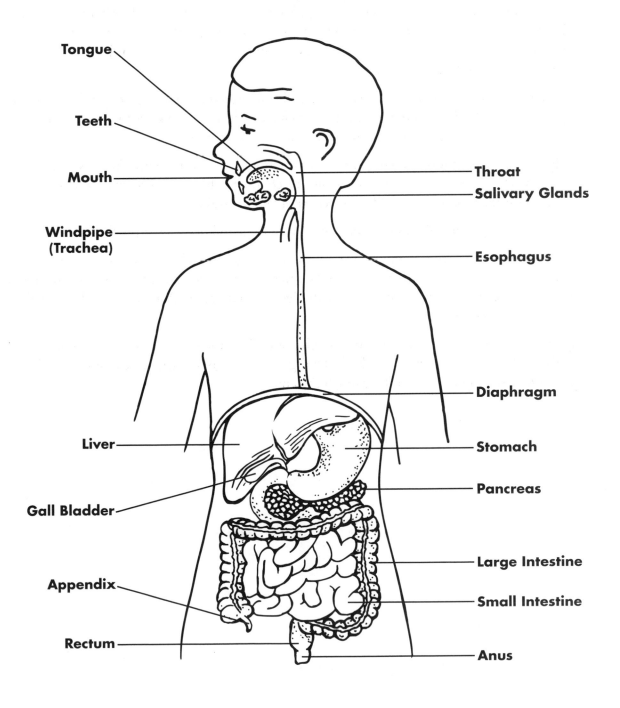

Tongue

Teeth

Mouth

Windpipe
(Trachea)

Throat

Salivary Glands

Esophagus

Diaphragm

Liver

Stomach

Pancreas

Gall Bladder

Appendix

Large Intestine

Small Intestine

Rectum

Anus

How Peristalsis Works

A. Food moves from the mouth to the esophagus.

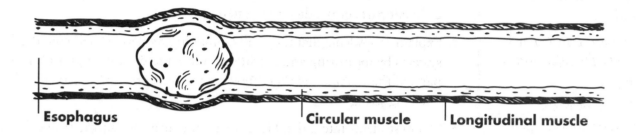

Esophagus　　　　　　　　　**Circular muscle**　　**Longitudinal muscle**

B. Circular muscles contract behind the food mass, while longitudinal muscles contract ahead of the food mass.

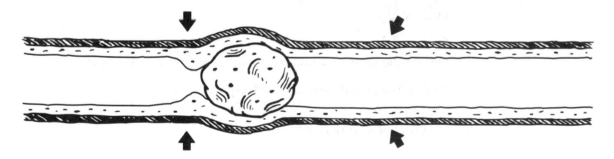

C. Muscle contractions force the food mass forward.

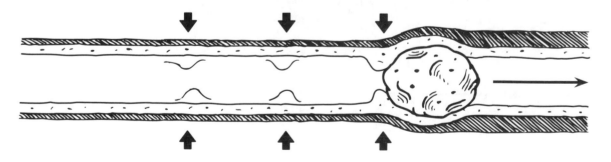

　　　　　　　　　18

Investigation 1

Measuring the Monstrous Digestive System

Materials

- student record sheets on pages 20 and 21, reproduced for each student
- overhead transparency of *The Digestive System* on page 17
- photocopy of the diagram for each pair of students
- measuring tools (rulers, metersticks)
- yarn (blue, red, green, yellow, and purple)
- scissors

Steps to Follow

1. Engage students in a discussion of why we need food. Lead them to the understanding that food and oxygen provide our cells with the energy they need to function. Display *The Digestive System* transparency and discuss the different parts of the digestive system.

2. Explain to students that they will be making models of their own digestive systems by measuring and cutting yarn to represent the lengths of different parts of the system, and then knotting the pieces of yarn together to form one long string.

3. Group students into pairs. Have them take turns measuring each other, so that each student has a set of data for his or her own body. Students should measure in centimeters.

4. Distribute student record sheets, diagrams, and materials. Either read the instructions together or have students complete the activity on their own.

Follow-Up

When students have completed the activity, hang the digestive system models around the room so the class can observe their actual length.

Review the record sheet answers, especially the Conclusions section. Students might say that the model showed them the length of the digestive system and the order of its different parts.

Measuring the Monstrous Digestive System

Procedure

1. Measure each part of the digestive system in centimeters. Record your data in the Observations section.

   • Digestion begins in the mouth, so measure and cut a piece of red yarn from the front to the back of the mouth. (You can do this by stretching the yarn from the front of your lips to the back of your jaw along your cheek.)

   • The esophagus is a tube that connects the mouth and stomach. Measure and cut a piece of blue yarn the length of the esophagus.* Tie the blue esophagus to the red mouth.

   • In the stomach, gastric juices break down solid food into a liquid. Find the length of the stomach by spreading the fingers of your hand and measuring the span from the thumb to the little finger. Measure and cut a piece of green yarn to match this length. Tie the green stomach to the blue esophagus.

   • The small intestine is the longest part of the digestive system. It is folded up inside of you so it fits. Food is further digested and absorbed here. Measure your height and multiply by four. Use yellow yarn to represent the length of the small intestine. Tie the yellow small intestine to the green stomach.

   • Last is the large intestine. It is much wider than the small intestine but much shorter. It is about as tall as you are. Undigested material from the small intestine moves to the large intestine before being excreted. Use purple yarn to represent the length of your large intestine. Then tie the purple large intestine to the yellow small intestine.

2. Add all the lengths together. This is the approximate length of your digestive system.

*The esophagus ends just below your rib cage.

Observations

Digestive Organ	Length (cm)
Mouth	
Esophagus	
Stomach	
Small Intestine	
Large Intestine	

Total Length of Digestive System: _____ cm

Conclusions

3. Why do you suppose your digestive system is so long?

_____

_____

4. A model is a representation of an object or a process or idea. It simplifies and helps to explain whatever it represents. List two things your model helped you learn about the digestive system.

_____

_____

_____

_____

Investigation 2

Pushing the Food Along

Materials

- student record sheet on page 23, reproduced for each student
- overhead transparency of *How Peristalsis Works* on page 18
- tubes, straws, pipes, and garden hoses of varying diameters
- stockings, socks, and pantyhose
- balls and other spheres of different sizes
- wires, twist-ties, rings, and other circular devices
- sclf-locking bags, pieces of cloth, buttons, and small paper clips
- petroleum jelly or other lubricant

Steps to Follow

1. Ask students, "What makes food move from the top to the bottom of the esophagus?" Students will probably say that gravity makes the food fall down. Then ask, "When giraffes bend their long necks down to drink water from a stream, how does the water move **up** through their necks?"

2. Tell students that it is not gravity but a process called **peristalsis** that moves food through the digestive tract. Explain that peristalsis is a combination of two types of muscle action. Lengthwise muscles push the food through the digestive system while circular muscles tighten and release the digestive tubes. Show students the *How Peristalsis Works* transparency.

3. Place students into small groups. Tell them that each group should make a model to show how peristalsis works using any of the available materials. They can squeeze a tennis ball through a stocking, holding their fingers in a ring-like shape to simulate the circular muscles and pushing to simulate the lengthwise muscles. They can lubricate a metal sphere, push it through a tube, and wrap a wire around the tube for the circular motion.

4. Tell the groups to decide how they want to make their models. Talk about brainstorming. Explain that in brainstorming no ideas are ridiculed. All ideas are recognized and recorded.

5. Have groups share their models with the class, explaining how their model simulates peristalsis with its two types of muscle action.

Follow-Up

Challenge students to swallow a mouthful of water while standing on their heads. Have them explain how water can "fall up" to their stomachs.

Pushing the Food Along

Procedure and Observations

1. What materials would you use for a model of how peristalsis works? Brainstorm with your group to get ideas. Listen respectfully. Write some suggestions below.

   _____

   _____

   _____

   _____

2. As a group, decide what materials you wish to use and how you will construct your peristalsis model. Gather the materials and build the model. Then discuss how you will present it to the class.

3. Describe your model below. Draw and label your model on the other side of this paper.

   _____

   _____

   _____

4. Compare your model with the actual peristalsis process. Discuss differences and likenesses.

   _____

   _____

   _____

Conclusion

5. Observe the other models. Which one(s) showed peristalsis most accurately? Explain why.

   _____

   _____

   _____

   _____

Investigation 3

Good-bye to Grease

Materials

- student record sheet on page 25, reproduced for each student
- trays to hold materials
- salad oil
- detergent
- medicine droppers
- toothpicks or coffee stirrers
- transparent glasses
- hand lenses
- water

Steps to Follow

1. Explain to students that they will conduct an investigation to discover what role bile plays in digestion. Explain that **bile** is a fluid that is produced by the liver and stored in the gall bladder. It is released into the small intestine when food is present.

2. Distribute the student record sheets and materials to small groups of students. Have students complete the investigation and record their observations and conclusions.

3. Have students share their observations and conclusions.

4. Lead students to understand that bile breaks down large blobs of fat into smaller blobs so that the body can digest it.

Follow-Up

Have students investigate whether detergents break down other common fatty substances such as butter or mayonnaise.

Good-bye to Grease

Procedure and Observations

1. Fill a glass about 3/4 full with water. Add four drops of oil and stir. Observe with a hand lens, and record your observations below.

   _____

   _____

2. What do you think will happen to the oil if you add some detergent and stir it?

   _____

   _____

3. Test your prediction. Fill another glass about 3/4 full with water. Add four drops of oil and stir. Add several drops of detergent. Observe the oil and detergent with a hand lens and record your observations below.

   _____

   _____

   _____

   _____

Conclusion

4. Bile acts like detergent. What can you conclude about the role of bile in digestion?

   _____

   _____

   _____

   _____

Good nutrition provides energy for cell growth and repair.

Prepare in Advance

Investigation 1: Have students keep track of and list everything they eat and drink in one 24-hour period. This data will be used in the investigation.

Teacher Information

Nutrients are the substances that the body needs in order to live. There are six types of nutrients (carbohydrates, fats, proteins, vitamins, minerals, and water) people should have each day. **Carbohydrates** (sugars and starches) and **fats** supply the body with energy; **proteins** are used to build, repair, and maintain the body; **vitamins** and **minerals** are needed to maintain bones and teeth and to keep the cells healthy; **water** is necessary for all body processes.

The USDA food pyramid was put together by scientists, physicians, nutritionists, and other health workers who researched medical journals, hospital records, health statistics, and other reports to determine the diets of people who live the longest and healthiest lives. The pyramid shape indicates that people need to eat more foods at the bottom of the pyramid than at the top. On a daily basis, people should eat 6 to 11 servings from the bread and pasta group, 3 to 5 servings from the vegetable group, 2 to 4 servings from the fruit group, 2 to 3 servings from the dairy group, 2 to 3 servings from the protein group, and a minimal amount of fats and sweets. Athletes and adolescent boys need the maximum number of servings, while sedentary people need the minimum.

Nutrients for Good Health

Nutrient	Why Needed	Where Found
Carbohydrates	energy, fiber	bread, cereal, pasta, fruit, rice
Proteins	repair, growth, make amino acids	milk, meat, fish, poultry, eggs, seeds, beans
Fats	energy	butter, meat, oil
Vitamins	strong bones and teeth, blood clotting, night vision, nerves, digestion, skin	fruits, vegetables, proteins, milk
Minerals	fluid balance, nerve transmission, strong bones and teeth	fruits, vegetables, protein products
Water	chemical reactions, fluid replacement	in most foods

USDA Food Guide Pyramid

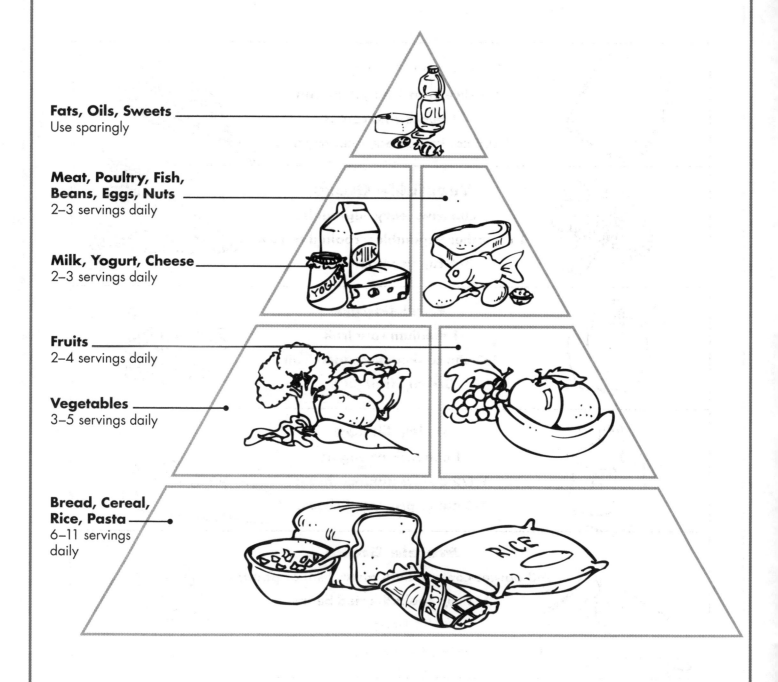

Fats, Oils, Sweets ———
Use sparingly

**Meat, Poultry, Fish,
Beans, Eggs, Nuts** ———
2–3 servings daily

Milk, Yogurt, Cheese ———
2–3 servings daily

Fruits ———
2–4 servings daily

Vegetables ———
3–5 servings daily

**Bread, Cereal,
Rice, Pasta** ———
6–11 servings
daily

What's in a Serving?

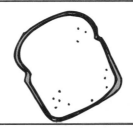 **Bread and Cereal Group**

1 slice bread, bagel, or bun

1 ounce cold cereal

1 cup cooked cereal, rice, or pasta

 **Vegetable Group**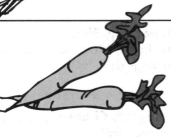

1 cup raw, leafy vegetables

1 cup other vegetables, cooked or raw

3/4 cup vegetable juice

 **Fruit Group**

1 medium raw fruit

1/2 cup cooked or canned fruit

3/4 cup fruit juice

 **Dairy Group**

1 cup milk or yogurt

1 1/2 ounces natural cheese

1/2 ounce processed cheese

Protein Group

2–3 ounces cooked, lean meat, fish, or poultry

1/2 cup cooked, dried beans

1 egg

5 tablespoons peanut butter

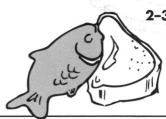  

Investigation 1

Plan a Real Meal

Materials

See advance preparation on page 26.

- student record sheet on page 31, 3 copies per student
- transparencies of the three charts *Nutrients for Good Health, USDA Food Guide Pyramid,* and *What's in a Serving?* on pages 27–29
- photocopies of the three charts for each group
- crayons or markers
- large manila drawing or construction paper

Steps to Follow

1. Before beginning the activity, have students keep track of and list everything they eat and drink in a 24-hour period.

2. Using the *Nutrients for Good Health* transparency, hold a discussion about nutrients.

3. Display the *USDA Food Guide Pyramid* transparency. Explain how and why the pyramid system was designed and why it is a pyramid shape.

4. Display and discuss the *What's in a Serving?* transparency.

5. Distribute copies of the three charts.

6. Place students in groups of four to share their 24-hour food lists. Have them compare their lists with the food pyramid and decide whether they had a nutritious day.

7. Distribute manila paper to all students. Have them divide it into three sections and label the top of each section "Breakfast," "Lunch," and "Dinner." Tell students to design a one-day food plan consisting of three meals and two snacks. Have them plan meals that they like to eat but that also meet the USDA guidelines for a healthful diet.

8. Display the food plans around the room. Distribute the record sheets to students and have them analyze their classmates' food plans.

9. Hold a discussion about the food plans and the USDA guidelines.

Follow-Up

Have students examine the school lunch menu for a week and analyze where it meets the USDA nutritional requirements and where it falls short.

Plan a Real Meal

Classmate's Name _____

Number of Servings from Each Food Group					
Breads	Veggies	Fruits	Dairy	Protein	Fats/Sweets

Based on the USDA guidelines, would you say this student planned a nutritious day? _____

Explain:

_____

_____

_____

Classmate's Name _____

Number of Servings from Each Food Group					
Breads	Veggies	Fruits	Dairy	Protein	Fats/Sweets

Based on the USDA guidelines, would you say this student planned a nutritious day? _____

Explain:

_____

_____

_____

Investigation 2

Testing Foods for Nutrients

Materials

- student record sheet on page 33, reproduced for each student
- iodine solution
- trays to hold materials
- droppers
- plastic dishes
- plastic knives
- small brown paper bags
- peanut butter
- bread
- potato slices
- lettuce leaves
- crackers
- fruit slices
- cheese slices or cubes
- newspaper

Steps to Follow

1. Make an iodine solution by mixing about one part iodine to four parts water. Use iodine that has **not** had the color removed.

2. Review nutrients and their importance. Emphasize that fats and carbohydrates (sugars and starch) supply the body with energy.

3. Tell students that they will test foods for starch by dabbing iodine on them. If a food contains starch, it will turn blue-black. They will then rub the food on a piece of brown paper bag and hold the bag up to the light. After any water dries, if the food contains fat, the bag will become translucent (allow light to shine through).

4. Place students in small groups. Have them cover their work tables with newspaper.

5. Distribute student record sheets, and then read them together. Have students complete their predictions individually.

6. Distribute a tray of materials to each group. Under your direction, have the class test the cracker for starch and for fat following steps 3 and 4 on the record sheet. Then have students record the information on their data tables.

7. Each group should test the other foods in the same manner and complete their record sheets.

8. Share class findings in a follow-up discussion.

Follow-Up

Have students bring in other foods to test.

Name _____

Testing Foods for Nutrients

Predictions

1. Which of the foods listed in the table below do you think contain starch? Give a reason for your prediction.

   _____

   _____

2. Which foods do you think contain fat? Give a reason for your prediction.

   _____

   _____

Procedure

3. Test the cracker for starch. Put a piece of cracker in a dish. Put a drop of iodine solution on the cracker. Did it turn blue-black? If so, it contains starch. Record your observations below.

4. Test the cracker for fat. Rub the cracker on a piece of a paper bag and hold the bag up to the light. Is there a translucent spot on the bag? If so, it contains fat. Record your observations below.

5. Test each of the other foods listed below. Record your data.

	Cracker	Bread	Potato	Peanut Butter	Cheese	Fruit	Lettuce
Contains Starch?							
Contains Fat?							

Conclusion

6. If you wanted to reduce your fat intake, which foods would you eat less of? Justify your answer by referring to your data table.

   _____

   _____

The heart and lungs work together.

Prepare in Advance

Investigation 2: Gather 2-liter plastic soft drink bottles (one per two students). Cut the bottoms off the bottles.

Teacher Information

The **circulatory** and **respiratory systems** work together to supply cells of the body with food and oxygen. The **heart** pumps oxygenated blood to the body. It pumps unoxygenated blood to the **lungs.**

The heart is divided into four chambers: the right and left atrium and the right and left ventricle. Blood flows through the chambers in a very specific manner. Special valves prevent the blood from flowing the wrong way.

Blood from the body enters the right atrium of the heart through the superior and inferior vena cava. Because this blood is full of carbon dioxide, it is dark red in color. The blood moves from the right atrium to the right ventricle. From there it is pumped through the pulmonary arteries to the lungs. In the lungs, the blood picks up oxygen and becomes bright red.

From the lungs, the bright red oxygenated blood moves back to the heart through the pulmonary veins. It enters the left atrium, and is pumped to the left ventricle. From there it is pumped out into the body through the aorta.

Breathing is the movement of air in and out of the respiratory system. The **diaphragm** and rib cage control breathing. The diaphragm is a large sheet of muscle beneath the chest. The ribs are the soft, curved bones that protect the heart and lungs. During inhalation, the diaphragm moves down and the ribs move up and out. This process increases the size of the chest and air is forced into the lungs. During exhalation, the diaphragm moves up and air is forced out the lungs.

The Heart and Lungs

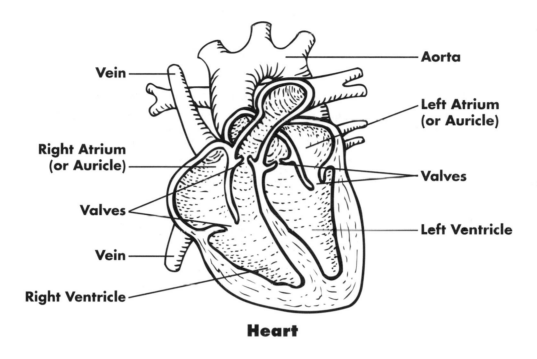

Vein

Aorta

Left Atrium (or Auricle)

Right Atrium (or Auricle)

Valves

Valves

Left Ventricle

Vein

Right Ventricle

Heart

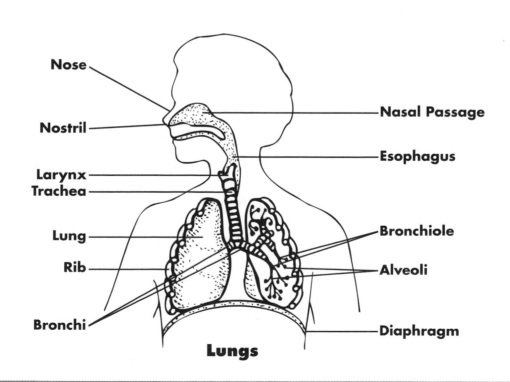

Nose

Nostril

Larynx
Trachea

Lung

Rib

Bronchi

Nasal Passage

Esophagus

Bronchiole

Alveoli

Diaphragm

Lungs

The Human Body • EMC 877

Investigation 1

The Circulatory System

Materials

- student record sheet on page 37, reproduced for each student
- overhead transparency of *The Heart and Lungs* on page 35
- white or light-colored butcher paper, large enough to trace a student
- bright red and dark red yarn
- clear tape
- scissors

Steps to Follow

1. Tell students that they will be making life-size human figures showing how blood moves through the body.

2. Show students the transparency of the heart. Hold a heart diagram against your body, so students understand the placement of the right and left labels.

3. Distribute student record sheets and read aloud the passage about blood circulation. As you are reading, have a student use a pointer to trace the path of the blood on the transparency. Repeat this process several times.

4. Place students in groups of four and give a piece of butcher paper to each group.

5. Have different students in each group do the following:

   - Stretch out, face up, on the butcher paper.

   - Trace the stretched-out person.

   - Cut out the traced outline.

   - Draw the lungs and heart on the body outline.

   - Reread the passage about blood circulation.

   - Tape the dark red yarn on the figure to show how unoxygenated blood flows from the body, to the right side of the heart, and then to the lungs.

   - Tape the bright red yarn on the figure to show how oxygenated blood flows from the lungs, to the left side of the heart, and then out to the body.

6. Have students use their life-size figures to explain to the class how blood is circulated through the heart, lungs, and body. Students should understand that the blood circles through the body, delivering oxygenated blood to all parts of the body before going back for more oxygen.

Follow-Up

Try to locate a life-size model of the circulatory system by asking your health or life science colleagues. Have students trace the path of blood through these models.

Name _____

Concept

5

The Human Body

Investigation 1

The Circulatory System

Procedure

1. Trace one member of your group and cut out the paper figure.

2. Draw a simplified version of the heart and lungs on the figure.

3. Read the passage below on blood circulation.

Blood Circulation

Blood from the body enters the right atrium of the heart. This blood is dark red, because it is full of carbon dioxide. The atrium contracts and blood is forced into the right ventricle. The ventricle contracts and moves the blood to the lungs. In the lungs, the blood gets oxygen and becomes bright red.

From the lungs, the bright red blood moves into the left atrium. The atrium contracts and forces the blood into the left ventricle. The ventricle contracts and the blood flows out to the body.

simplified heart

Right Atrium	Left Atrium
Right Ventricle	Left Ventricle

simplified lungs

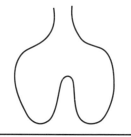

4. Tape the dark red yarn on the figure so that it shows the path of unoxygenated blood through the heart and lungs.

5. Tape the bright red yarn on the figure so that it shows the path of oxygenated blood through the heart and lungs.

Conclusion

6. Why is "circulatory" a good name for this system?

_____

_____

_____

_____

©2002 by Evan-Moor Corp.   37   The Human Body • EMC 877

Investigation 2

Breathing Balloons

Materials

- student record sheet on page 39, reproduced for each sudent
- overhead transparency of *The Heart and Lungs* on page 35
- 2-liter plastic soft drink bottles with the bottoms cut off
- small balloons
- large balloons
- rubber bands

Steps to Follow

1. Show students the overhead transparency of the lungs. Explain what happens to the lungs and diaphragm during inhalation and exhalation.

2. Tell students to put their hands on their ribs in order to feel the way the rib cage moves up and out during inhalation and down and in during exhalation.

3. Group students in pairs. Tell them they will be making a model of the respiratory system to show how this process works.

4. Have students stretch the neck of the small balloon around the top of the bottle, so that the balloon hangs down inside like a lung. Tell them to secure the large balloon with a rubber band.

5. Students should then cut off the top of the other balloon and stretch it across the bottom of the bottle like a diaphragm, also securing it with a rubber band.

6. Tell students to hold the bottom balloon and pull it gently several times, watching what happens to the balloon inside the bottle.

7. Have students share their observations and conclusions with the class. Students should observe that when they pull down on the diaphragm, the lung expands. When they let go of the diaphragm, the lung deflates.

8. Help students conclude that pulling the rubber band is like stretching the diaphragm. Both cause inflation of the lungs. Letting go of the rubber band is like relaxing the diaphragm. Both cause deflation of the lungs.

Follow-Up

Have students draw diagrams of their respiration models during the inhalation and exhalation phases.

Name _____

Concept

5

The Human Body

Investigation 2

Breathing Balloons

Procedure

1. Stretch the neck of the small balloon around the top of the bottle, so that the balloon hangs down inside. Secure the balloon with a rubber band. This balloon represents a lung.

2. Cut off the top of the large balloon and stretch it across the bottom of the bottle, also securing it with a rubber band. This balloon represents the diaphragm.

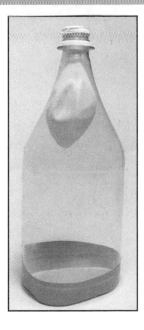

3. Before you do the next step, make a prediction. What do you think will happen to the lung if you pull down on the diaphragm?

_____

_____

_____

Observations

4. What happens to the lung when you pull down on the diaphragm?

_____

_____

5. What happens to the lung when you let go of the diaphragm?

_____

_____

Conclusion

6. How is your model like an actual respiratory system?

_____

_____

_____

Investigation 3

Clogged Arteries

Materials

- student record sheet on page 41, reproduced for each student
- containers
- trays to hold materials
- butter
- olive oil
- bacon grease

Steps to Follow

1. Melt butter and bacon grease so that they are both in liquid form. Warm the olive oil until it is approximately the same temperature as the other oils.

2. Prepare a tray for each group of four students. On each tray, place a small container of melted butter, liquid bacon grease, and olive oil. Label the containers.

3. Tell students that they will be observing what happens to different types of fat when they sit overnight. Distribute record sheets and discuss. Tell students that they will be making two sets of observations on three types of fat, one observation today and another observation after the fats have sat overnight.

4. Have students record their observations on their record sheets.

Follow-Up

Students should understand that animal and other saturated fats can clog arteries. Discuss the health issues associated with excess animal and other saturated fats: clogging of the arteries, possibly leading to heart disease.

Clogged Arteries

Procedure and Observations

1. Observe the three containers of fat. Describe each one.

   Butter:

   _____

   Bacon Grease:

   _____

   Olive Oil:

   _____

2. What do you think each oil will look like once it cools?

   _____

3. Let the containers sit in a cool place overnight. Observe and describe each one again.

   Butter:

   _____

   Bacon Grease:

   _____

   Olive Oil:

   _____

Conclusion

4. Digested fats are carried around in your blood. Based on your observations in this experiment, which fats do you think would be most likely to clog up your arteries? Support your conclusion with evidence from the investigation.

   _____

   _____

   _____

Muscles and bones provide movement and support.

Prepare in Advance

Investigation 1: Gather enough materials so that each pair of students can make a model arm. The models consist of two cardboard tubes jointed by a ball at the "joint." Experiment with materials you have available until you find a tube/ball combination that works. (You might try empty toilet paper tubes, but craft tubes of a smaller diameter and thicker walls work better. Try Ping-Pong balls, other small balls, or even a plastic Easter egg for the joint.) See page 45 for an example of what the finished model could look like.

The night before the investigation, glue balls to the ends of half of the cardboard tubes, one for each pair of students. Put the model arm together according to the directions on page 45. Familiarize yourself with how the model works so that you can help students construct and understand their models.

Investigation 2: Ask students to wear comfortable clothes and athletic shoes. Do not allow them to participate in this activity if it will cause them physical harm. If your room is small, make arrangements to use another area.

Teacher Information

Bones and **muscles** work together to support the body and allow it to move. Muscles are attached to bones by strong bands of tissues called tendons. When muscles contract, they cause the attached bones to move. For example, when the biceps muscle contracts, it causes the elbow to bend, raising the lower arm. While the biceps muscle is contracting, the triceps muscle at the back of the upper arm is relaxing.

There are two groups of muscles—voluntary muscles, which you can control, and involuntary muscles, which work automatically. Leg muscles are voluntary muscles, while those that line the digestive tract are involuntary.

Bones serve other functions as well. They protect vital organs, store fat, and produce blood cells. Although bones are hard, they are composed of cells and contain blood vessels. Like other body parts, they need food and oxygen to function.

Major Muscles of the Body

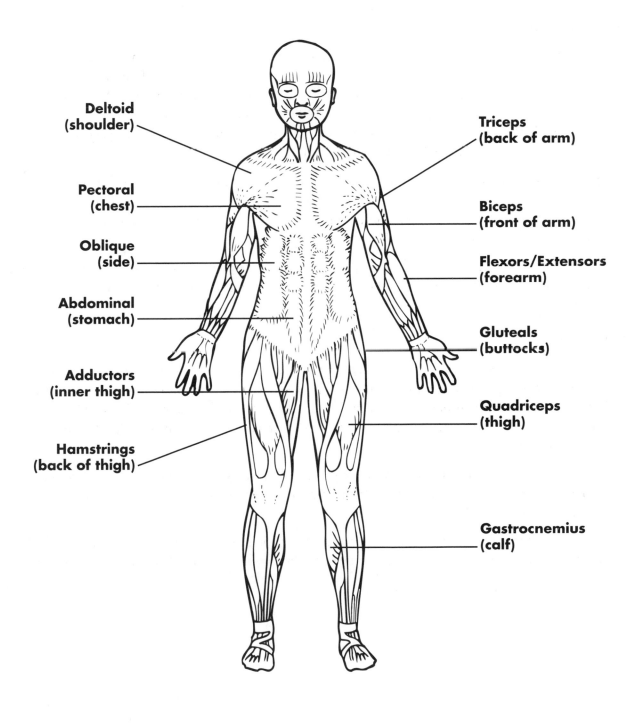

Deltoid
(shoulder)

Pectoral
(chest)

Oblique
(side)

Abdominal
(stomach)

Adductors
(inner thigh)

Hamstrings
(back of thigh)

Triceps
(back of arm)

Biceps
(front of arm)

Flexors/Extensors
(forearm

Gluteals
(buttocks)

Quadriceps
(thigh)

Gastrocnemius
(calf)

Investigation 1

Muscles Work in Pairs to Move Bones

Materials

See advance preparation on page 42.

- *Making the Model Arm* instructions on page 45, reproduced for each pair of students

- overhead transparency of the *Major Muscles of the Body* on page 43

- Ping-Pong balls or other balls

- cardboard tubes

- long rubber bands

- paper clips

- pushpins

- masking tape

- tacky glue

- rulers

Steps to Follow

1. Show students the *Major Muscles of the Body* transparency. Point out the **biceps** and **triceps** muscles.

2. Tell students to let their right arm hang down and feel the biceps muscle on the front of the upper arm. Then bend this arm at the elbow to feel the biceps muscle contract.

3. Have students place their left hand on the triceps muscle on the back of the upper arm. Have them move their arm down toward the floor and feel the triceps muscle contract.

4. Emphasize that muscles work in pairs, one contracting as the other relaxes.

5. Pair students and distribute the model materials and record sheets. Each pair will need one ball, two cardboard tubes, two rubber bands, two paper clips, and one pushpin.

6. Explain to the class that they will be constructing a model arm that shows how the biceps and triceps muscles work together to move the arm. Hand out the *Making the Model Arm* instruction sheet. Using the model you made and the instruction sheet, show students how to construct their model arms.

7. Have students bend and straighten the model arm and notice what happens to the biceps and triceps muscles (rubber bands). (As the muscles contract, they shorten. As the muscles relax, they lengthen.) Have students record their observations on their record sheets.

8. Encourage students to experiment with pulling on the biceps and triceps rubber bands. What do they notice about the movement of the arm? (Students should note that the arm bent when they pulled on the biceps rubber band, and straightened when they pulled on the triceps rubber band.)

9. Students should conclude that this investigation shows that arm muscles work in pairs—as one muscle (rubber band) contracts, the other relaxes.

Follow-Up

Have students feel their thigh when bending and straightening their leg to observe how another set of muscles works in pairs.

Making the Model Arm

1. Measure down 3 cm on one end of each tube. Using the pushpin, poke a hole on each side. (Figure A)

2. Straighten the paper clips. Push them through the holes. Fold the ends toward the open ends of the tubes. (Figure B)

3. Loop a rubber band around the bent paper clips on **one** tube. Wrap tape around the tube to hold the clips down. (Figure C)

4. Place the tubes together as shown in Figure D. Loop the rubber bands around the paper clips on the other tube. Tape the paper clips down.

5. Tape the rubber band to the lower arm as shown. Tape the other rubber band to the "joint" as shown. (Figure D)

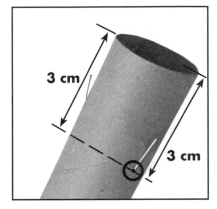

Figure A

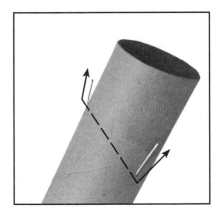

Figure B

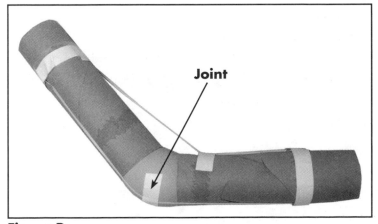

Joint

Figure D

Figure C

Name _____

Muscles Work in Pairs to Move Bones

Procedure

1. Follow the instructions on the *Making the Model Arm* sheet to construct the model arm.

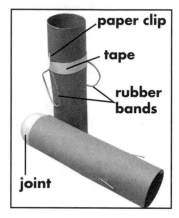

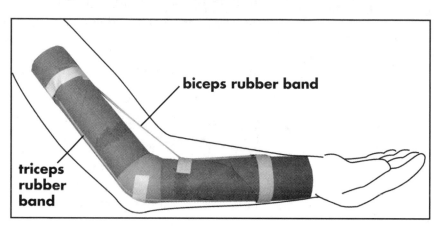

2. What do you think will happen to the biceps muscle when you bend the arm?

    _____

3. What do you think will happen to the triceps muscle when you straighten the arm?

    _____

Observations

4. Bend the arm. Describe what happens to the biceps muscle.

    _____

5. Straighten the arm. Describe what happens to the triceps muscle.

    _____

Conclusion

6. How does this investigation show that muscles work in pairs?

    _____

    _____

    _____

Investigation 2

Finding Your Muscles

Materials

See advance preparation on page 42.

- student record sheets on pages 48 and 49, reproduced for each student
- *Major Muscles of the Body* diagram on page 43, reproduced for each student
- 1-lb (0.45 kg) weights or cans of food

Steps to Follow

1. Distribute copies of the *Major Muscles of the Body* diagram. Go over the diagram with the students, instructing them to feel the various muscles on their body as you point them out on the chart.

2. Explain to the class that they will be doing exercises to distinguish one muscle from another, and then determine how each one feels as it moves.

3. Have students do the exercises described on the record sheets together under your supervision. Or, place students in small groups and have them work at their own pace.

4. After each exercise, students should use the *Major Muscles of the Body* diagram to identify the name of the muscle or muscles they were working. They should record the muscle names on their record sheets.

5. Don't be too concerned if students do not identify the correct muscle for each exercise. This activity is designed to acquaint students with the location of some muscles and to observe how these muscles feel and work.

6. Go over student answers together. Have students explain why they selected the muscles they did.

Answer Key

1. gastrocnemius (calf muscle, back)
2. quadriceps
3. abdominals
4. deltoids, biceps, triceps
5. pectorals, deltoids, triceps
6. hamstrings (thigh muscle, back)
7. adductors
8. obliques
9. gluteals, quadriceps

Follow-Up

Have the physical education teacher give the class a demonstration of which muscles students use when playing their favorite sports.

Name _____

Finding Your Muscles

Procedure

Perform each exercise. Then write the name of the muscle(s) you think you were using.

Observations

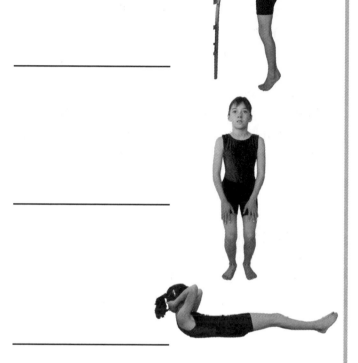

1. Toe Raises

Stand with feet flat on the floor, holding a table or chair for support. Rise up on your toes as high as you can. Lower yourself slowly.

_____

2. Partial Squats

Support yourself between two chairs if necessary. Bend your legs until you feel pressure on your thighs. Straighten up completely.

_____

3. Crunches

Lie on your back, flat on the floor. Place hands behind your neck for support. Keeping the small of your back on the floor, raise your head and shoulders off the floor. Lower your head and shoulders.

_____

4. Military Press

Sit on a chair with a weight in each hand. Place hands on your thighs, palms up. Bending your arms at the elbows, raise the weights to shoulder level. Then straighten your arms and raise the weights to arm length over your head. Pause and return to starting position.

_____

5. Push-ups

Lie facedown and place hands flat on the floor at shoulder level, about two feet apart. Bend your knees, cross your ankles, and extend your arms, so that you are resting on your hands and knees. Lower yourself by bending your arms, until your chest almost touches the floor. Then straighten your arms and return to your original position.

_____

6. Leg Curl

Lie facedown with your legs straight. Bend your knees and bring your heels toward your backside. Straighten your legs again.

_____

7. Side Lunge

Stand with legs apart. Bend forward at the waist and place hands in front of you on the floor, toes facing outward. Bend at the right knee and press toward the right leg. Repeat on the left side.

_____

8. Torso Twist

Stand with legs apart and knees slightly bent. Place hands on shoulders, elbows out to the side. Keeping hips and knees stiff, do a complete twist from side to side.

_____

9. Upward Squeeze

Stand with legs apart, hands on hips. Bend your knees and lower your body several inches. Slowly return to start, squeezing buttocks as you rise.

_____

The Human Body • EMC 877

Investigation 3

Terribly Tired Muscles

Materials

- student record sheet on page 51, reproduced for each student
- spring-type clothespins
- stopwatches or a clock with a second hand

Steps to Follow

1. Group students into pairs. Explain that they each will squeeze a clothespin for 30 seconds, count and record the number of squeezes, and then take a 10-second rest. They will do this a total of four times, squeezing for 30 seconds and resting for 10 seconds.

2. Distribute record sheets and materials. Tell students to squeeze the clothespin a few times just to see how it feels. Have them record their predictions before they begin their actual tests.

3. Emphasize that for a fair test, students should hold and squeeze the clothespin the same way (squeezing very hard) all four times.

4. Discuss conclusions. Tell students that when muscles are used extensively, muscle fatigue or soreness develops.

Follow-Up

Talk about other muscles that become sore when overused. Suggest that students plan and carry out their own muscle fatigue investigation. They can do biceps curls, squats, or a similar activity. Allow them to change their investigation in some way in order to get better results. Have them make predictions and construct charts for recording their data.

Terribly Tired Muscles

Prediction

1. How do you think your squeezing speed will change after you squeeze the clothespin for a while?

_____

Procedure

2. Work with a partner who will time you. Squeeze a clothespin for 30 seconds, counting and recording the number of squeezes. Then take a 10-second rest. **Do not rest for more than 10 seconds.**

3. Repeat this procedure three more times, and then switch places with your partner.

Observations

Number of Clothespin Squeezes in 30 Seconds

	Squeezer:	Squeezer:
First Time		
Second Time		
Third Time		
Fourth Time		

Conclusions

4. Was your prediction correct?

_____

5. How did continuous squeezing affect your muscles?

_____

_____

_____

The nervous system relays messages to and from the brain.

Prepare in Advance

Investigation 1: Borrow stopwatches from the physical education teacher or other source.

Investigation 2: Prepare four tasting solutions for each group and label the containers "salty," "sweet," "bitter," and "sour."

Teacher Information

The **nervous system** consists of the **brain,** the **spinal cord,** and the **nerves** that reach throughout the body. Messages from the nerves are channeled to the spinal cord. Many are then sent on to the brain. Conversely, messages are handed down from the brain and spinal cord to the nerves.

There are three main parts to the brain: the medulla, which controls involuntary activities such as breathing and digestion; the cerebellum, which coordinates movement and maintains balance; and the cerebrum, which controls thought, memory, and learning. All conscious acts are recorded in the cerebrum. Scientists believe that these experiences establish pathways or connections in this part of the brain and that these pathways are reinforced through similar experiences. Hence, repetition enhances learning.

The brain gets information from the **sense organs.** The five sense organs—the eyes, the ears, the nose, the skin (the largest organ in the body), and the taste buds—get information from the outside world and send it to the spinal cord and brain via nerves. The brain and spinal cord then send out messages of their own, instructing the body on how to react to a stimulus.

One of our sense organs is located on the tongue—tiny bumps called taste buds. When we eat, bits of dissolved food get into the taste buds through openings called pores. Inside each taste bud is a nerve ending. This nerve transmits information to the brain. The brain then tells us what we are tasting. Human tongues can distinguish four kinds of tastes: sweet, salty, sour, and bitter. Certain areas of the tongue are more sensitive to one category of taste than to another.

Nerve cells in the skin enable us to detect pain, pressure, and temperature. The receptors for pain are located near the surface of the skin, while those for pressure are located deeper in the skin. Some areas of the body, such as fingertips, have more touch receptors than others and are therefore more sensitive.

 The Human Body • EMC 877

Four Identical Mazes

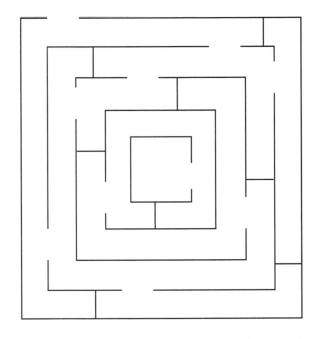 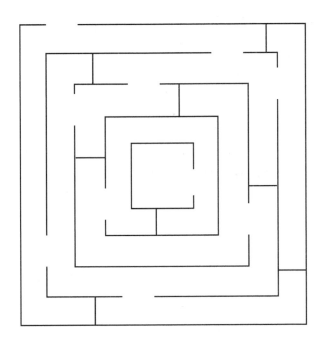

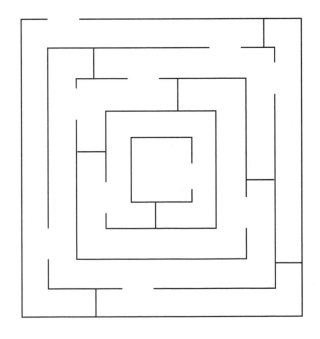 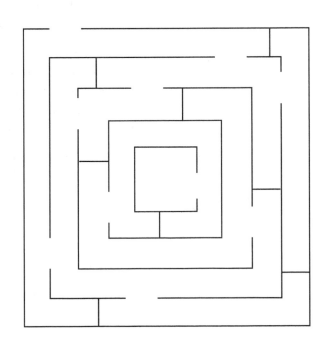

Investigation 1

Practice Makes Perfect

Materials

See advance preparation on page 52.

- student record sheet on page 55, reproduced for each student
- *Four Identical Mazes* on page 53, reproduced for each student
- stopwatches or a clock with a second hand
- graph paper
- colored pencils

Steps to Follow

1. Pose these questions to the class: "How did practicing affect something you were trying to improve, such as keyboarding on a computer or playing ball? Did you ever get faster at something by practicing?"

2. Tell students that the cerebrum is the part of the brain that controls thought, memory, and learning. Point out that scientists believe that our experiences make connections in the cerebrum, and that repetitions strengthen the connections.

3. Explain to students that they will go through a paper and pencil maze four times to determine whether or not their speed increases.

4. Group students into pairs. Distribute record sheets and go over the procedures.

5. Have partners time each other and record the data.

6. On a large sheet of graph paper, draw a graph like the one here. Point out the title and the two labels. Indicate that the y (vertical) axis is used for the number of seconds and the x (horizontal) axis is used for the four trials. Show students how to plot the data using different colors for each person. Distribute graph paper and help students construct similar graphs using their own data.

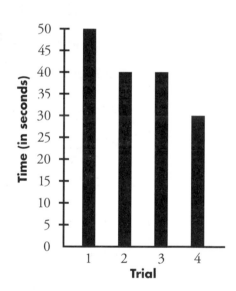

7. Hold a class discussion comparing data from each pair of students. Stress the importance of using numbers to support conclusions.

Follow-Up

Have students plan another investigation to determine whether practice improves learning for another skill.

Name _____

Practice Makes Perfect

Prediction

1. How do you think practice will affect the time it takes you to complete a maze?

_____

Procedure

2. Time a partner to find out how long it takes for him or her to go through a maze. Your partner will do the maze four times.

3. Record the data below.

4. Reverse roles, with you as the maze-doer and your partner as the timer. Again, record the data.

5. Use your data to create a bar graph of your results. Your teacher will show you how to make the graph.

Observations

Time It Takes to Get Through Maze

Student _____	Student _____
Trial 1: _____ (sec)	Trial 1: _____ (sec)
Trial 2: _____ (sec)	Trial 2: _____ (sec)
Trial 3: _____ (sec)	Trial 3: _____ (sec)
Trial 4: _____ (sec)	Trial 4: _____ (sec)

Conclusion

6. How does practice affect the speed at which you can perform a skill? Support your conclusion with data.

_____

_____

_____

Investigation 2

Taste Bud Road Map

Materials

- student record sheet on page 57, reproduced for each student
- trays to hold materials
- newspapers
- dissolved solutions of salt, sugar, and instant coffee
- concentrated lemon juice
- paper cups
- cotton swabs
- water

Steps to Follow

1. Tell students that they are able to taste food because of tiny bumps on their tongue called **taste buds.** Explain that nerves inside the taste buds send information to the brain, telling them what they are tasting.

2. Inform students that they will be investigating the areas on their tongue that are sensitive to the four types of taste: sweet, salty, sour, and bitter. They will investigate by having a partner swab their tongue with four solutions.

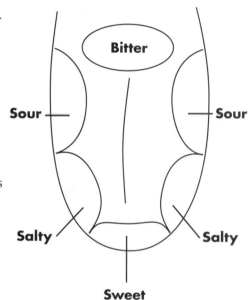

3. Group students into pairs. Have them cover their tables with newspaper. Distribute trays of materials and read the record sheets together. Guide students as they begin, and have them complete the activity at their own pace.

4. Caution students to dip only clean swabs into the solutions to avoid the spread of germs. Have them discard swabs after one use.

5. Record the class data on a chart. Before students write their conclusions, discuss results.

Follow-Up

Have students conduct the same investigation with their noses plugged so they can determine whether smell affects the way food tastes.

Taste Bud Road Map

Procedure

1. Take a sip of water, swish it around in your mouth, and swallow it. Close your eyes. Have your partner dip a swab in one of the solutions and touch the tip, middle, edges, and back of your tongue. Decide where you taste that solution. Label that area with the name of the solution on "My Tongue Map" below.

2. Follow the same procedure for the other three solutions. Rinse your mouth with water between each swabbing.

3. Trade places with your partner and swab your partner's tongue.

4. Look at the data on the class chart. Write your conclusion and label the "Class Tongue Map."

Observations

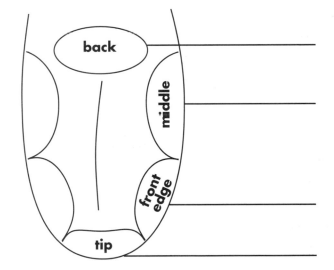

My Tongue Map

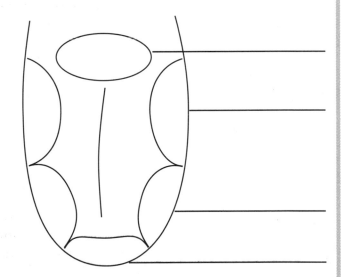

Class Tongue Map

Conclusion

5. Do all parts of your tongue detect sweet, salty, sour, and bitter tastes? Support your conclusion with evidence from your experiment.

_____

_____

_____

Investigation 3

Locating Your Touch Receptors

Materials

- student record sheets on pages 60 and 61, reproduced for each student
- blindfolds
- small paper clips
- colored pencils

Steps to Follow

1. Prepare the paper clips by opening them up and forming them into a U-shape.

2. Tell students that they are able to feel things because of special nerve cells in the skin. Explain that the nerve endings for light touch are located just beneath the surface of the skin. Help students to understand that some areas of the body are more sensitive because they have more touch receptors and the receptors are very close together.

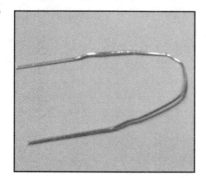

3. Inform students that they will be investigating which area of the arm and hand is most sensitive to touch—the back of the hand, the fingertip, the palm, or the wrist. Tell them they will be gently touching their partners ten times on each area with either one or two points of a paper clip. Emphasize that an area is most sensitive if subjects are able to determine the correct number of points that are touching them.

4. Group students into pairs. Read the student record sheet together with the class to be sure students understand what to do. Distribute clips and blindfolds (or tell students to close their eyes) and have students conduct the first part of the activity, recording their answers on the table on their record sheets.

5. Before students start their graphing, explain how they can set up a double bar graph to display their data. You may want to draw a sample graph (see sample on page 59) on the board and have students follow along using their own data.

Touch Sensibility Data

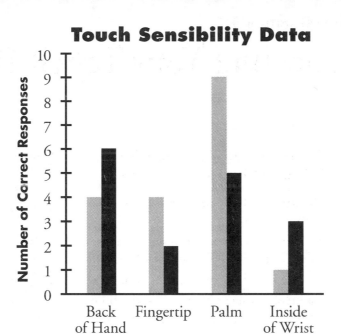

Sue ■ Juan

6. Review standards for a graph. Emphasize that TAILS is a useful acronym to help students remember the components of a good graph.

    Title
    Axes
    Increments
    Labels
    Scale

    The **title** should tell an uninformed reader what the investigation is about.

    The independent (changed) variable should be placed on the y (vertical) **axis**. The dependent variable should be placed on the x (horizontal) **axis**.

    Increments should be equal. Units should be evenly spaced.

    Each axis of the graph should have a **label**. Each label should describe what is being represented on that axis.

    The **scale** should reflect the range of numbers represented by the data. For example, students should not label the y axis from 1 to 100 if the largest data number is only 15.

7. Discuss results. Be sure students understand that the most sensitive area is the one that had the most correct responses.

Follow-Up

This is a good activity to use as an assessment. Use TAILS to grade the graph. Students' conclusions should be based on which areas were the most sensitive (had the most correct responses). To get full credit for the conclusion section, students should cite actual numbers.

Name _____

Locating Your Touch Receptors

Prediction

1. Which area do you think is most sensitive to touch—the back of the hand, the fingertip, the palm, or the inside of the wrist?

_____

Procedure

2. Work with a partner, one person as the subject and the other as the investigator.

3. As the subject, wear a blindfold and place one hand on the desk, palm down.

4. As the investigator, **gently** touch the subject on the back of the hand with either one or two points of the clip.

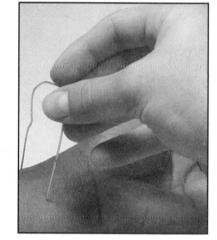

5. Ask your partner, "How many points did you feel?" If the response is correct, make a tally mark next to the words "Back of Hand" on the table below. If the response is not correct, don't write anything. Touch your partner on the back of the hand nine more times for a total of ten, varying between one and two points.

6. Repeat this process with the fingertip, palm, and inside of wrist.

7. Reverse roles. Again, record the data on the table.

Observations

Tally of Correct Responses	
Investigator: _____	Investigator: _____
Subject: _____	Subject: _____
Back of Hand	Back of Hand
Fingertip	Fingertip
Palm	Palm
Inside of Wrist	Inside of Wrist

8. Follow your teacher's instructions to plot your data on a bar graph. Use one color for your results and another for your partner's.

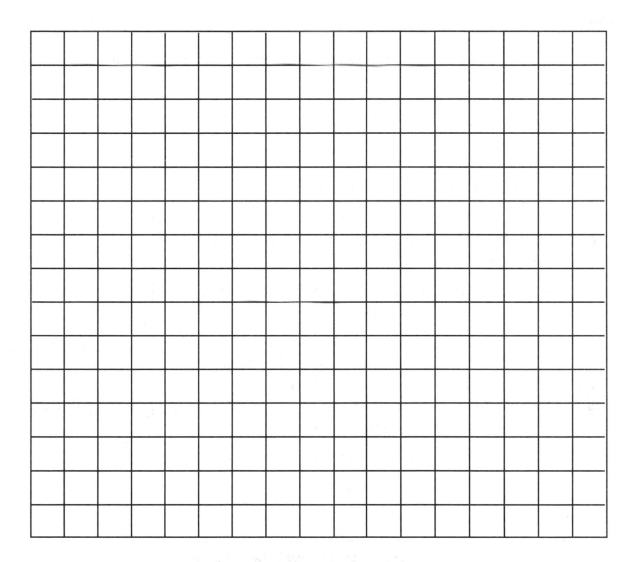

Conclusion

9. Which area was most sensitive to touch? Support your conclusion with actual data from the table or graph.

_____

_____

_____

Parents pass traits to future generations.

Prepare in Advance

Investigation 1: Collect one nickel and one penny for each student.

Teacher Information

Chromosomes are structures inside the nucleus of a cell that contain genetic material called **DNA.** Information about an organism's physical traits is stored in the DNA. Physical traits are passed from one generation to the next through chromosomal DNA.

Each chromosome contains many pairs of **genes.** A gene is a segment of DNA that specifies a specific trait in an organism. One gene often determines more than one trait, and some traits are controlled by more than one gene.

Humans have 23 pairs of chromosomes. In 22 chromosomes the pairs are identical, but one chromosome, the one responsible for determining the sex of a child, is different. In the sex-determining chromosome, females have two X chromosomes (XX) and males have one X and one Y chromosome (XY). During reproduction, the sex cells divide and the baby gets one chromosome from each parent. The baby always gets an X chromosome from the mother. If the baby gets an X chromosome from the father, it's a girl, but if the baby gets a Y chromosome from the father, it's a boy.

The basic laws of heredity were discovered by a monk named Gregor Mendel. Mendel did experiments with pea plants. He found that certain traits of pea plants, such as tallness, were dominant, and other traits, such as shortness, were recessive. Dominant traits are those that produce visible traits. When Mendel crossed tall and short pea plants, he found that all of the offspring were tall.

A **Punnett square** can be used to show how traits are passed to the next generation. Remember that each gene comes in a pair. Each version of the gene is called an **allele.** An allele may be dominant or recessive. In a Punnett square, uppercase letters denote dominant alleles and lowercase letters denote recessive alleles. When the alleles are alike (two dominant or two recessive) we call the trait **pure.** When the alleles are unalike (one dominant and one recessive) we call the trait **hybrid.**

The letters on the top of the square stand for the alleles of one parent for a particular gene. The letters on the left side of the square stand for the alleles of the other parent for the same gene. The allele pairs of the four offspring are shown in the center of each square.

	B	**B**
b	**Bb**	**Bb**
b	**Bb**	**Bb**

Punnett Squares

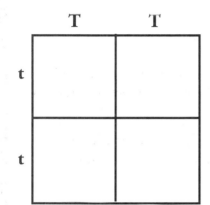

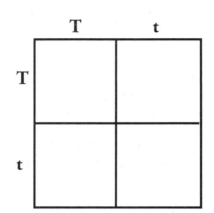

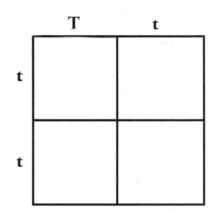

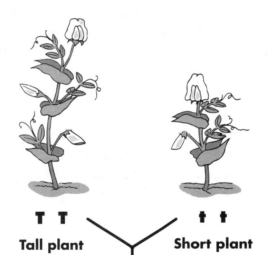

T T
Tall plant

t t
Short plant

T t
Tall plant

Investigation 1

A Girl or a Boy?

Materials

See advance preparation on page 62.

- student record sheet on page 65, reproduced for each student
- pennies
- nickels
- masking tape
- permanent marking pens

Steps to Follow

1. Hold a discussion about what determines the sex of a child. Explain that each parent contributes a piece of genetic material called a chromosome. Women donate only X chromosomes, but men donate either an X or a Y chromosome. When the chromosomes join, XXs form girls while XYs form boys, so the male chromosome determines the sex of the baby.

2. Place students in groups of four. Tell students they will conduct an activity to determine the chances of having a boy or a girl. Each student will work alone, but will pool his or her data at the end of the investigation.

3. Give each student a nickel, a penny, and some tape. For the female, they should mark an X on both sides of the nickel. For the male, they should mark an X on one side of the penny and a Y on the other side.

4. Emphasize that since each family has four children, they must flip both coins four times for each family (36 times altogether). Be sure students have four tally marks for each family.

5. Do the first family, the Bonos, together with the class. Help them mark their charts.

6. Have them continue on their own for the other eight families.

7. Students should total their tally marks and pool data with the other students in their group. Students should find that about 50% of the children are girls and about 50% are boys. Explain that "about" half does not have to be exactly 18 boys and 18 girls. Findings of 16 or 20 are still about half.

8. Discuss results. Record all students' data on a class chart so they can see how percentages get closer to 50/50 the larger the sample.

Follow-Up

Have students research how many boy and girl babies are born each year in the United States or the world. With a sample size this large, students will see how close to 50/50 the percentages really are.

Name _____

A Girl or a Boy?

Prediction

1. Do you think there's an equal chance of having a boy or a girl?

_____

Procedure

2. Put masking tape on each side of a penny and a nickel.

3. The nickel will be the female. Females have two X chromosomes, so write X on both sides.

4. The penny will be the male. Males have one X and one Y chromosome, so write X on one side and Y on the other side.

5. Start with the Bonos. Flip both coins. If they land on XX it's a girl, so make a tally mark in the "Girl" box. If they land on XY it's a boy, so make a tally mark in the "Boy" box. The Bonos are having a total of four children, so flip the coins three more times to determine the sex of the other three Bono children. Record your results.

6. Repeat this procedure for the other families. Each family has four children, so flip both coins four times for each family. Record your results.

Observations

Number of Girls and Boys in 9 Families of Four									
Sex of Baby	**Bono**	**Doe**	**Blake**	**Cohen**	**Riley**	**Favio**	**Baku**	**Khan**	**Min**	**Total**
Girl									
Boy									

Conclusions

7. What do you notice about the total number of girls and boys on your chart?

_____

8. On your group's chart?

_____

9. On the class chart?

_____

Investigation 2

Dominant and Recessive Traits

Materials

- student record sheets on pages 67 and 68, reproduced for each student

Steps to Follow

1. Discuss dominant and recessive traits. Explain that brown eyes are dominant and blue eyes are recessive, so if one parent has "pure" brown eyes and the other parent has "pure" blue eyes, all of the children will have brown eyes. Tell students that the genes for blue eyes are still in the children's cells, but they are not seen.

2. Distribute record sheets and have students read the pairs of traits at the top of the page. Tell students to observe their classmates and predict which trait in each pair they think is dominant and which is recessive.

   Note: The dominant trait in the population at large is underlined.

eyes: blue <u>brown</u>	tongue: <u>roller</u> nonroller
hair: <u>dark</u> blond	dimples: yes <u>no</u>
hair: <u>curly</u> straight	ear lobes: attached <u>unattached</u>

3. Have students count the number of students with each trait and use tally marks to record the information on the chart.

4. Have students use the grid provided to graph their data. Help them as needed.

5. Discuss class results.

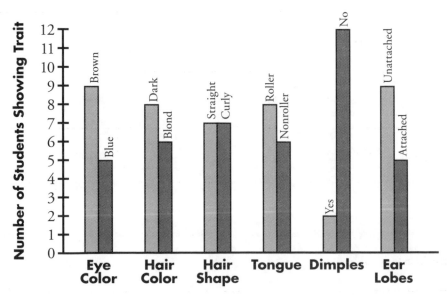

Sample Class Data for Dominant and Recessive Traits

Dominant and Recessive Traits

eyes: blue or brown	**tongue:** roller or nonroller
hair: dark or blond	**dimples:** yes or no
hair: curly or straight	**ear lobes:** attached or unattached

Prediction

1. Which of the above traits do you think are dominant?

   _____

Procedure and Observations

2. Study your classmates to determine which traits they have.

   _____

3. Use tally marks to record your findings on the chart below.

   _____

Tally of Students with Each Trait		
Eyes	Blue	Brown
Hair	Dark	Blond
Hair	Curly	Straight
Tongue	Roller	Nonroller
Dimples	Yes	No
Ear Lobes	Attached	Unattached

4. Use the grid below to create a bar graph of your data.

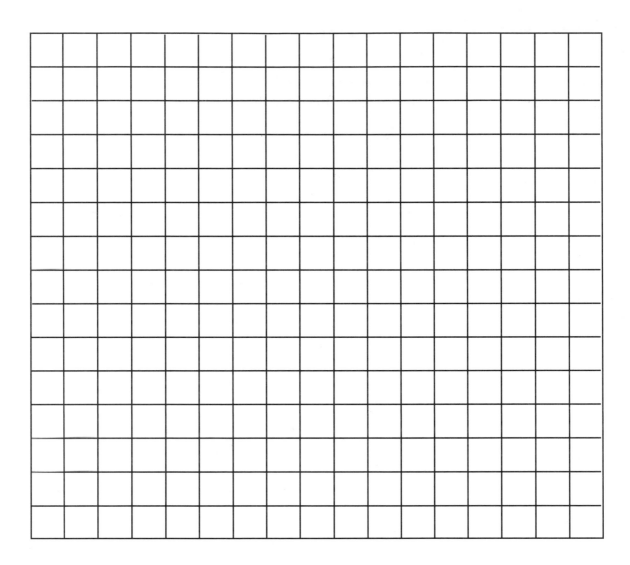

Conclusion

5. Which traits do you think are dominant? Support your conclusions with data.

_____

_____

_____

_____

Concept 8 — **The Human Body**

Investigation 3

Punnett Squares

Materials

- student record sheets on pages 70 and 71, reproduced for each student
- overhead transparency of *Punnett Squares* on page 63

Answer Key (page 71)

Step 3

No children can be blue-eyed.

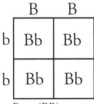

Pure (BB) parent
Pure (bb) parent

Step 5

The odds of having a blue-eyed child are 50%.

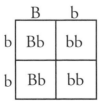

Hybrid (Bb) parent
Pure (bb) parent

Steps to Follow

1. Tell students that Gregor Mendel was a monk who studied genetics by cross-pollinating pea plants. Mendel knew that when pea plants self-pollinated, the offspring of the tall plants were always tall and the offspring of the short plants were always short. He called these offspring "pure." When Mendel cross-pollinated tall and short pea plants, he expected some offspring to be short and some to be tall just like the parent plants. Instead he found that all the offspring were tall. He wondered why. Mendel called these tall plants "hybrids" because they had both tall and short parents. He discovered that some traits, like tallness, are dominant, and other traits, like shortness, are recessive. In hybrids, dominant traits are visible, while recessive traits are hidden.

2. Show students the *Punnett Squares* transparency for pea plants on page 63. Explain that the uppercase letter *T* stands for the dominant trait of tallness and that the lowercase letter *t* stands for the recessive trait of shortness.

3. Distribute record sheets and go over the first set of Punnett squares (tall and short pea plants) together. Have students fill in the Punnett squares for tall and short pea plants on their record sheets as you do them on the overhead.

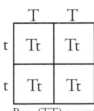

Pure (TT) parent
Pure (tt) parent

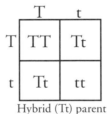

Hybrid (Tt) parent
Hybrid (Tt) parent

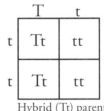

Hybrid (Tt) parent
Pure (tt) parent

4. Have students fill in the Punnett squares for pea plants with round *(R)* and wrinkled *(r)* seeds. Check their answers before continuing.

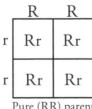

Pure (RR) parent
Pure (rr) parent

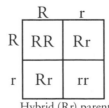

Hybrid (Rr) parent
Hybrid (Rr) parent

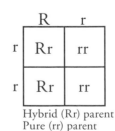

Hybrid (Rr) parent
Pure (rr) parent

5. Have students complete the record sheets on their own.

Punnett Squares

Procedure and Observations

1. Follow your teacher's instructions to complete the Punnett squares for tall and short pea plants. Tallness (T) is a dominant trait and shortness (t) is recessive.

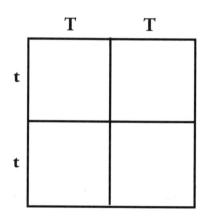 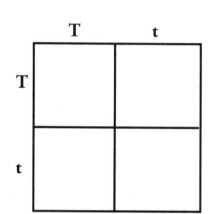 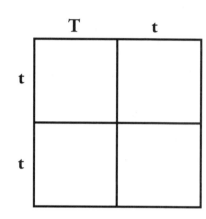

2. Complete the Punnett squares for pea plants with round (R) and wrinkled (r) seeds by yourself. Check your answers when you are finished.

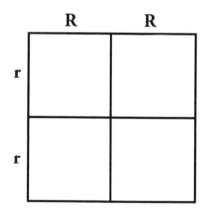

3. In eye color, brown is a dominant trait and blue is recessive. If one parent has brown eyes (BB) and one has blue (bb), what are the odds of them having a blue-eyed child?

_____

4. Complete the Punnett square to see if there could be any blue-eyed (bb) offspring.

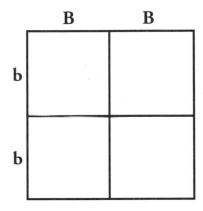

5. If one parent has brown eyes but is a hybrid (Bb), and the other parent has blue eyes (bb), what are the odds of them having a blue-eyed child?

_____

6. Complete the Punnett square to see if there could be any blue-eyed (bb) offspring.

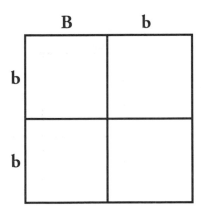

Conclusion

7. How do Punnett squares allow you to predict how traits are passed from one generation to the next?

_____

_____

Body systems interact.

Prepare in Advance

Investigation 1: Collect 2-liter soft drink bottles and cut off the bottoms, one per group of two to three students.

Investigation 2: Collect stopwatches (one for every four students) from the physical education teacher or other source.

Teacher Information

By now, students should have an understanding of the systems of the body. Emphasize that although they have been studying different systems, all the parts work together to keep the whole body alive and well. Use the following information for a review.

The body gets its energy from food and oxygen. Because food cannot be used in its original form, it must first be digested. The **digestive system** consists of the mouth, esophagus, stomach, and small intestine. In each of these organs, mechanical and chemical processes help digest the food. Digested food goes through tiny structures in the small intestine to the bloodstream where it is carried to all parts of the body. Waste products go to the large intestine where they are eliminated.

The **respiratory** and **circulatory systems** work together to provide oxygen to cells. Oxygen enters the body through the mouth and nose, travels down the trachea, and then goes to the lungs. The heart pumps blood to the lungs where it picks up oxygen. Oxygenated blood is transported to all parts of the body through the bloodstream. When the blood circulates through the kidneys, waste products are filtered out and sent to the bladder where they are excreted as urine.

The **skeletal** and **muscular systems** work together to allow the body to move. Some movements, such as walking or running, are voluntary, while others, such as the movement involved in breathing or digesting food, are involuntary.

The **nervous system** helps coordinate body functions by receiving information from the outside world via the senses, relaying the information to the spinal cord and brain, and then sending messages to different parts of the body as needed.

Human Body Systems

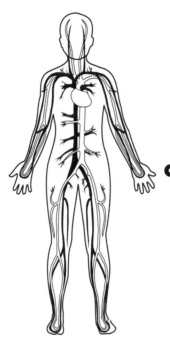

Cardiovascular

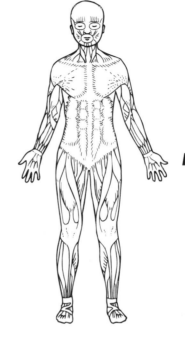

Muscular

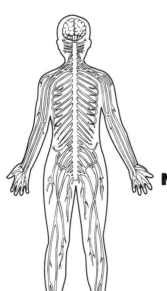

Nervous

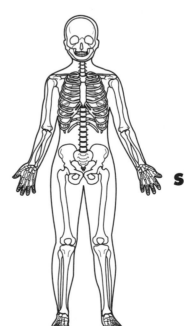

Skeletal

Investigation 1

The Blood–Kidney Connection

Materials

See advance preparation on page 72.

- student record sheets on pages 75–77, reproduced for each student
- 2-liter soft drink bottles with bottoms cut off
- fine and coarse sand
- soil
- spoons
- charcoal
- filter paper
- gravel
- rubber bands
- cheesecloth
- tumblers
- beakers
- funnels
- teaspoons
- rulers
- newspaper

Steps to Follow

1. Hold a class discussion about the kidneys and how they work. Tell students that to understand how the kidneys filter blood, they will make filtering devices to filter dirty water. Explain that each group of students will make its own filtration system and will test three types of filters to discover which one cleans the water the best.

2. Explain that in a well-designed investigation only one variable is changed while the others remain the same. Tell students that in their investigation, they will change the type of filter, but the other factors (amount of water poured in, how dirty the water is to start with, and the amount of filtering material in the system) will remain the same.

3. Distribute, read, and discuss the record sheets. Point out that students should give complete and accurate descriptions of the condition of the water. Place students in small groups and have them cover their work tables with newspaper. Then instruct them to proceed on their own.

4. Final question: Answers will vary, but students should state that the kidneys filter the blood so that waste products can be excreted from the body.

Follow-Up

Have students research where the kidneys are located in the body and how they are connected to the bladder.

The Blood–Kidney Connection

Procedure

1. To construct a filtration device, place a piece of cheesecloth around the top of a bottle, secure it with a rubber band, turn the bottle upside down, and set it inside a beaker. Make three devices like this.

2. Brainstorm with your group to determine the three kinds of filters you want to use in your filtration device. Fine sand, coarse sand, charcoal, gravel, and filter paper may be used as filters. Write your plan on the planning sheet below and show it to your teacher for approval.

3. Once you've received approval, gather your materials, test the three filters, and complete the record sheet.

Planning Sheet

Height (cm) of filtration material _____

Number of teaspoons of soil in the "dirty" water _____

Number of cups of water to pour through _____

Number of times to pour water through filter _____

Material and amount to be used:

Filter #1 _____

Filter #2 _____

Filter #3 _____

4. Which filter do you think will clean the water best? Why?

_____

_____

Observations

5. Describe in detail what the water looked like after using each filter.

Filter #1

_____

_____

_____

_____

Filter #2

_____

_____

_____

_____

Filter #3

_____

_____

_____

_____

Conclusion

6. Which filter worked the best? Justify your response with evidence from your observations.

_____

_____

_____

_____

_____

_____

Analysis

7. Name the variable that you changed in this investigation.

_____

_____

8. Name two things that you kept the same.

_____

_____

9. If you could repeat this investigation, what would you do to make the water even cleaner? Write a paragraph explaining what you would do and why you would do something different.

_____

_____

_____

_____

_____

_____

10. Explain why the kidneys are important to the body. In your explanation, describe how this investigation helped you to understand how the kidneys work.

_____

_____

_____

_____

_____

Investigation 2

The Heart–Lung Connection

Materials

See advance preparation on page 72.

- student record sheets on pages 79 and 80, reproduced for each student

- stopwatches or a clock with a second hand

Steps to Follow

1. Hold a discussion about how body systems work together. Examples: muscles pull on bones to cause movement; blood circulates through the heart and lungs.

2. Ask the class these questions: "If you're sleeping and breathing slowly, is your heart beating slowly too? What if you run for a mile and are breathing rapidly? Is your heart also beating fast?"

3. Tell students to design an investigation that looks at the connection between heart rate and breathing rate. Discuss how they might do this. Students might suggest taking a pulse rate and a breathing rate before and after exercising.

4. Show students how to take their pulse. Have them place four fingers of one hand on their neck as shown. Time the class together, so they get used to finding and counting their pulse. Some students may find it easier to take a pulse at the wrist. Have them place four fingers of one hand on the wrist of the other hand.

5. Show students how to time with a stopwatch. Tell them to set the watch at zero, push the start button, and, after 30 seconds, say "stop" while pushing the stop button. Have them practice before beginning their investigation.

6. Place students in groups of four, distribute record sheets, and have groups continue on their own. Circulate through the room, giving help when needed.

Follow-Up

Hold a science conference. Have groups describe their investigations and present their data as if they were scientists at a conference.

Name _____

The Heart–Lung Connection

Procedure

1. With your group, plan an investigation to determine whether heart rate and breathing rate are connected. Decide what you will do and discuss your plan with your teacher.

2. Once your teacher has approved your plan, list the steps below.

_____

_____

_____

_____

_____

_____

_____

_____

_____

_____

_____

_____

_____

_____

_____

_____

_____

Observations

3. Conduct your investigation. Your observations will probably include data, so create a data table in the space below. Ask your teacher for help with the table.

Conclusion

4. What did you learn about the connection between heart rate and breathing rate? Justify your conclusions with data.

_____

_____

_____

_____